HBCU Letter Tracing
LEARN ABC'S & HBCUs

OVER 100 INSTITUTIONS

HISTORICALLY BLACK COLLEGES & UNIVERSITIES

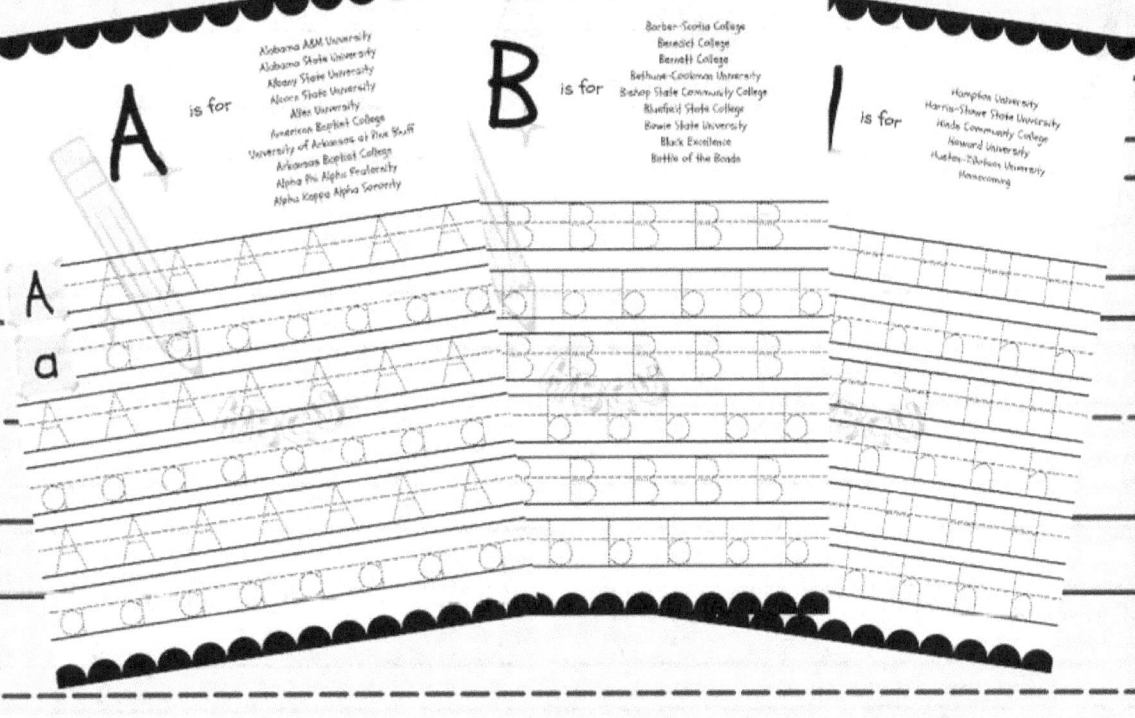

HANDWRITING NOTEBOOK FOR KIDS

AGES 3+

A is for

Alabama A&M University
Alabama State University
Albany State University
Alcorn State University
Allen University
American Baptist College
University of Arkansas at Pine Bluff
Arkansas Baptist College
Alpha Phi Alpha Fraternity
Alpha Kappa Alpha Sorority

B is for

Barber-Scotia College
Benedict College
Bennett College
Bethune-Cookman University
Bishop State Community College
Bluefield State College
Bowie State University
Black Excellence
Battle of the Bands

B B B B B B B

b b b b b b b b

B B B B B B B

b b b b b b b b

B B B B B B B

b b b b b b b b

B B B B B B B

b b b b b b b b

C is for

- Central State University
- Cheyney University of Pennsylvania
- Claflin University
- Clark Atlanta University
- Clinton College
- Coahoma Community College
- Concordia College
- Coppin State University

D is for

Delaware State University
Denmark Technical College
Dillard University
University of the District of Columbia
Delta Sigma Theta Sorority
Divine Nine

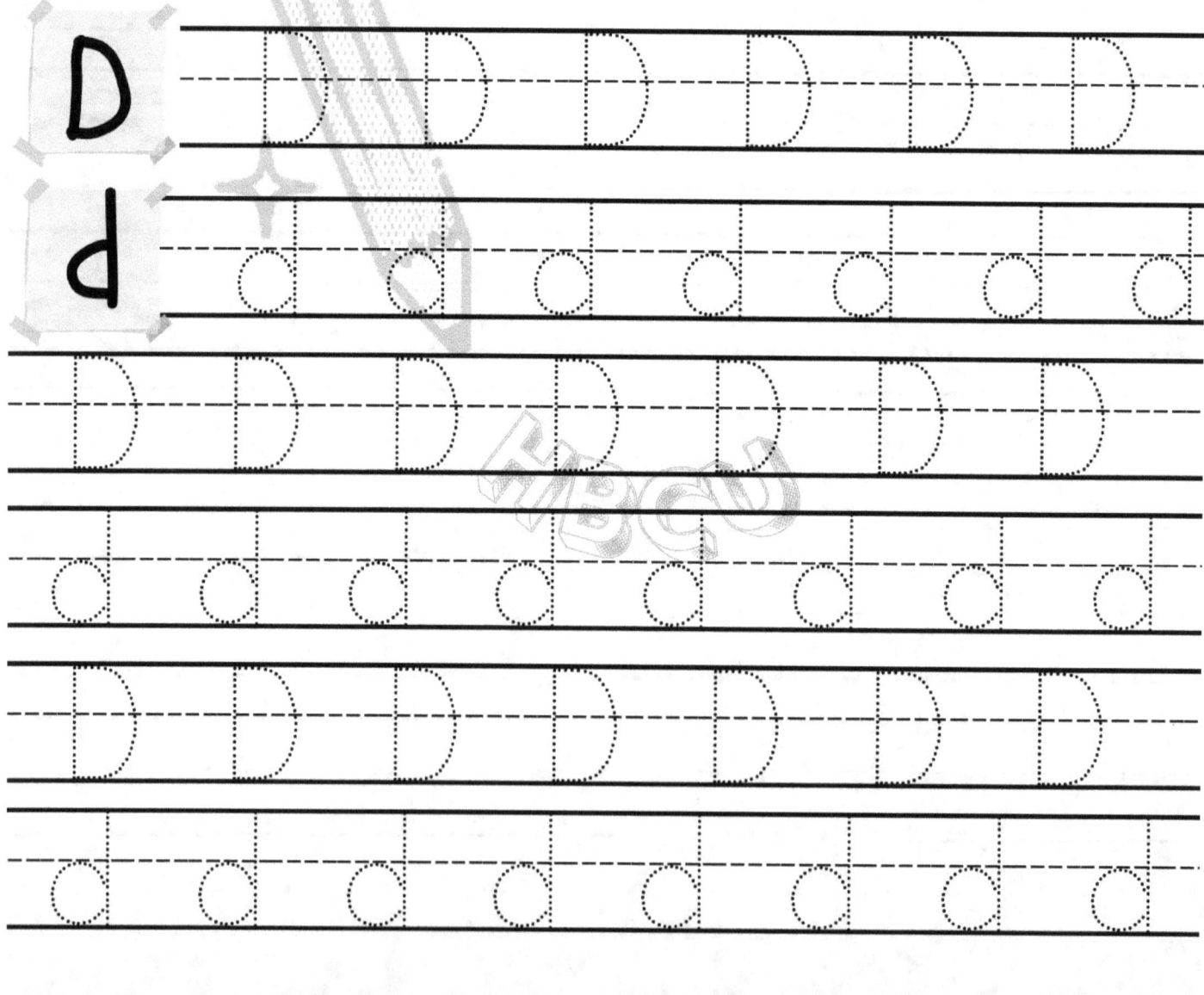

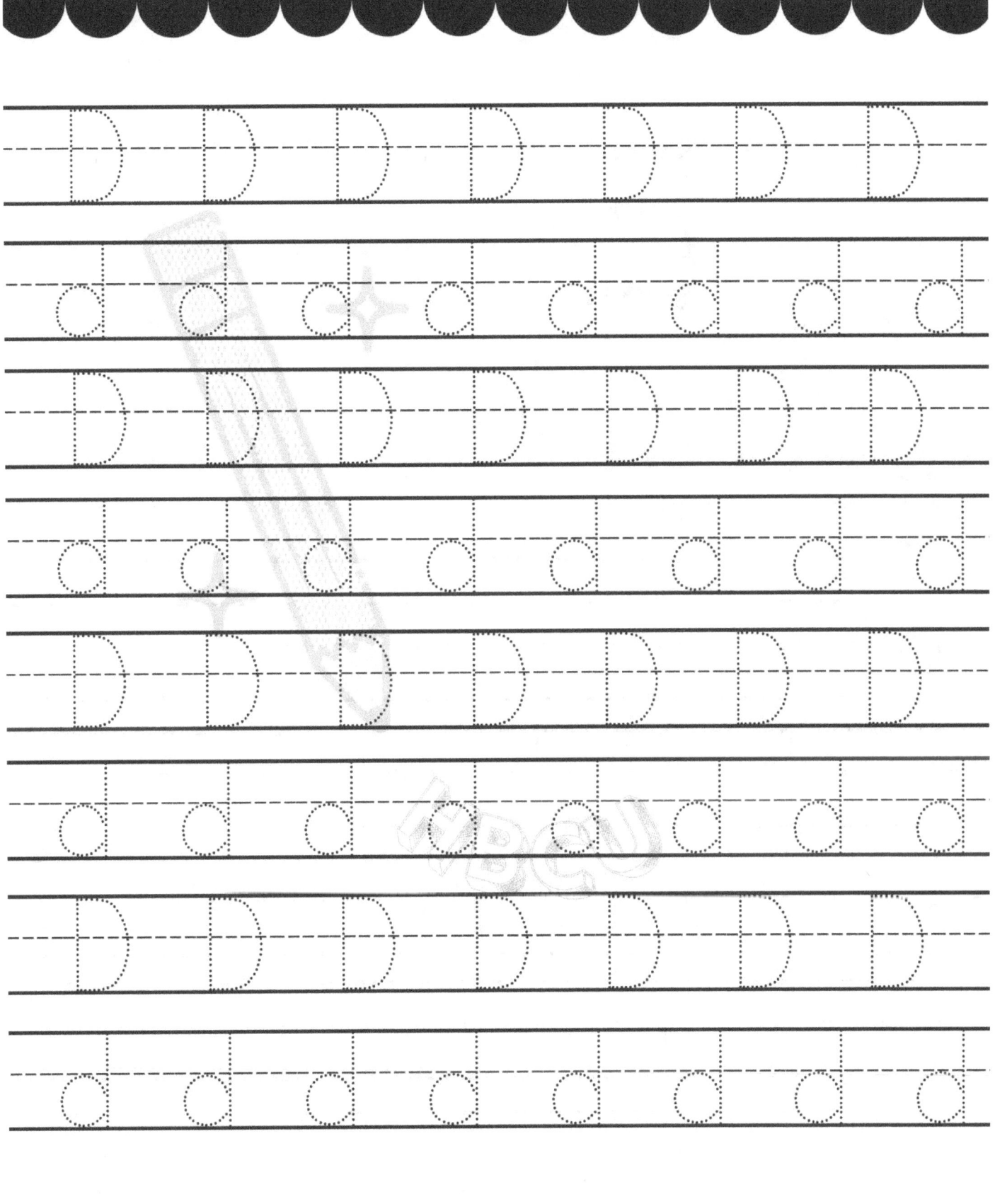

E is for Edward Waters University
Elizabeth City State University

F is for

Fayetteville State University
Fisk University
Florida A&M University
Florida Memorial University
Fort Valley State University

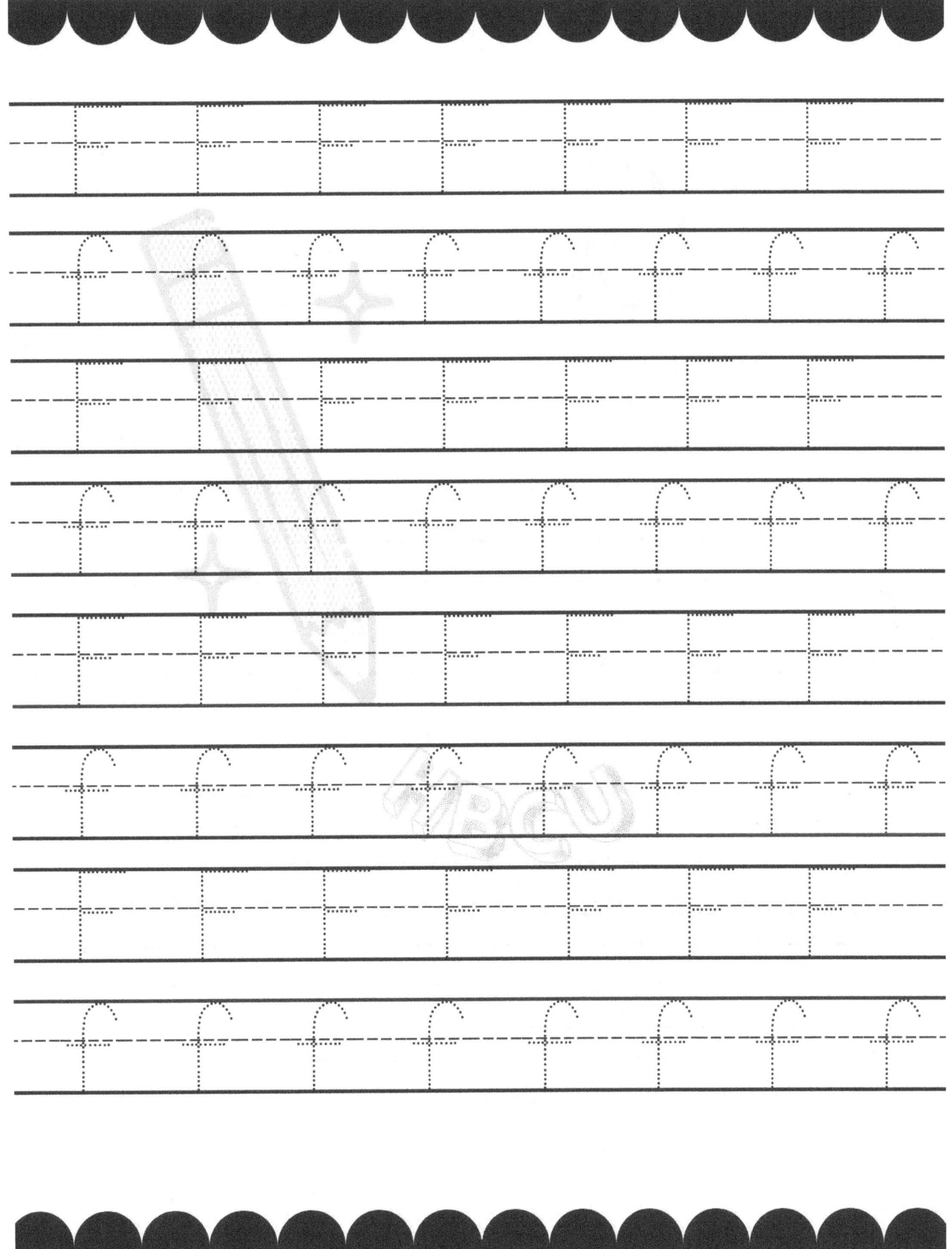

G is for Gadsden State Community College
Grambling State University

H is for

Hampton University
Harris-Stowe State University
Hinds Community College
Howard University
Huston-Tillotson University
Homecoming

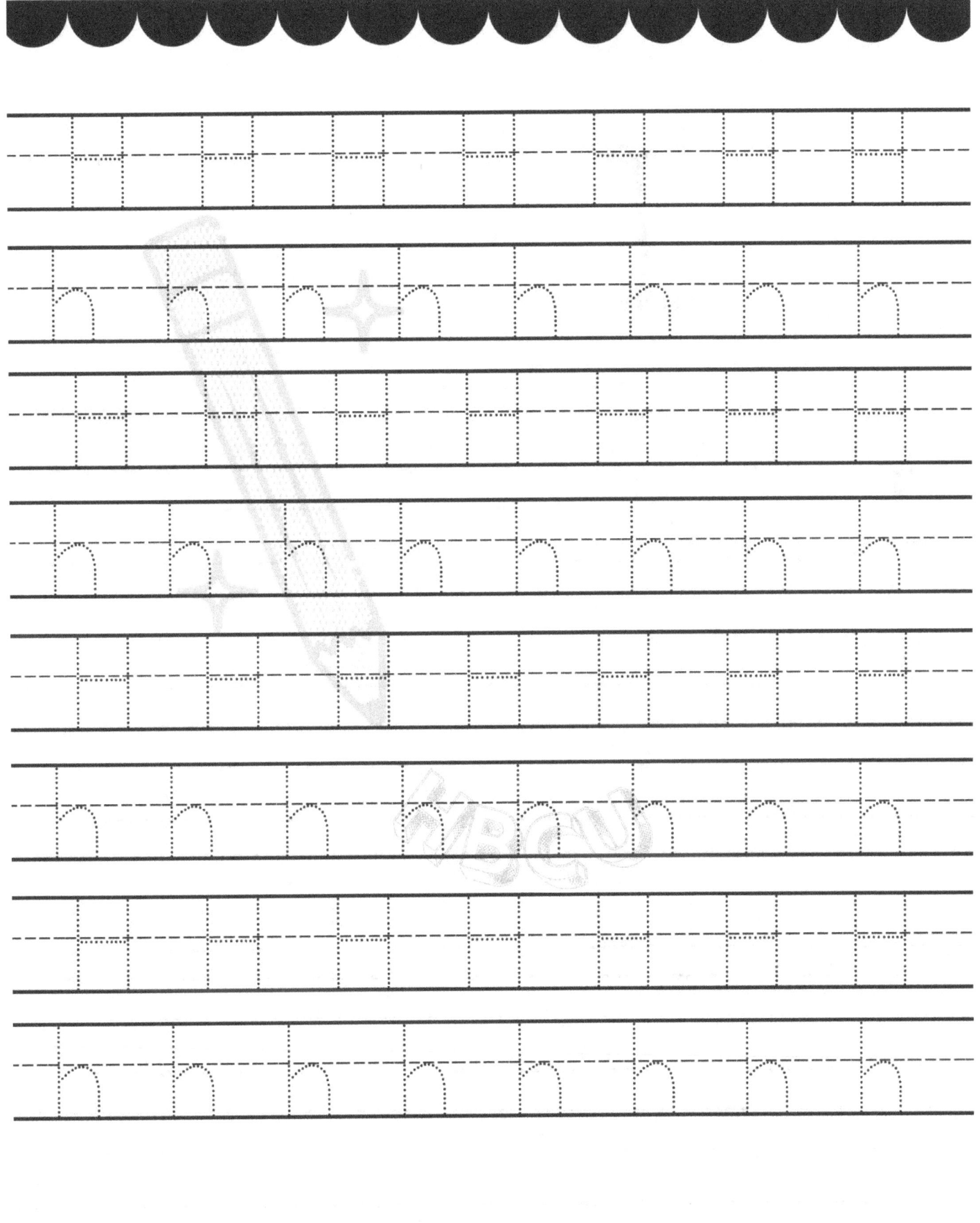

I is for Interdenominational Theological Center
Iota Phi Theta Fraternity
I love my HBCU

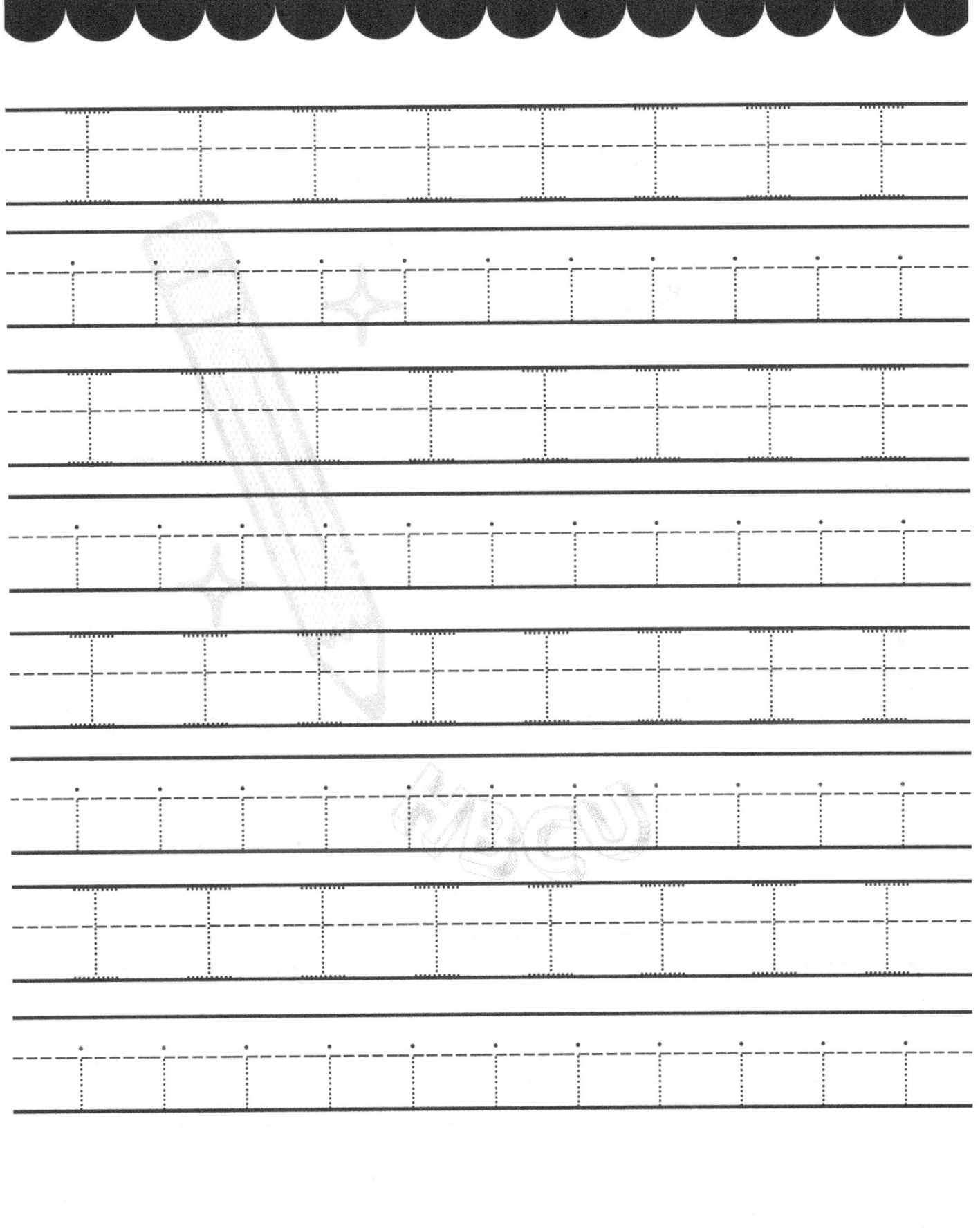

J 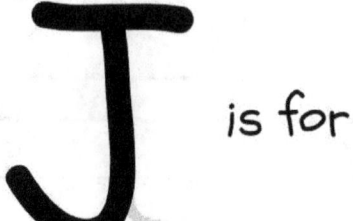 is for

J. F. Drake State Technical College
Jackson State University
Jarvis Christian College
Johnson C. Smith University

K is for

Kentucky State University
Knoxville College
Kappa Alpha Psi Fraternity
Kings

K K K K K K

k k k k k k

K K K K K K

K K K K K K

K K K K K K

K K K K K K K

L is for
Lane College
Langston University
Lawson State Community College
LeMoyne-Owen College
The Lincoln University
Lincoln University-Jefferson City

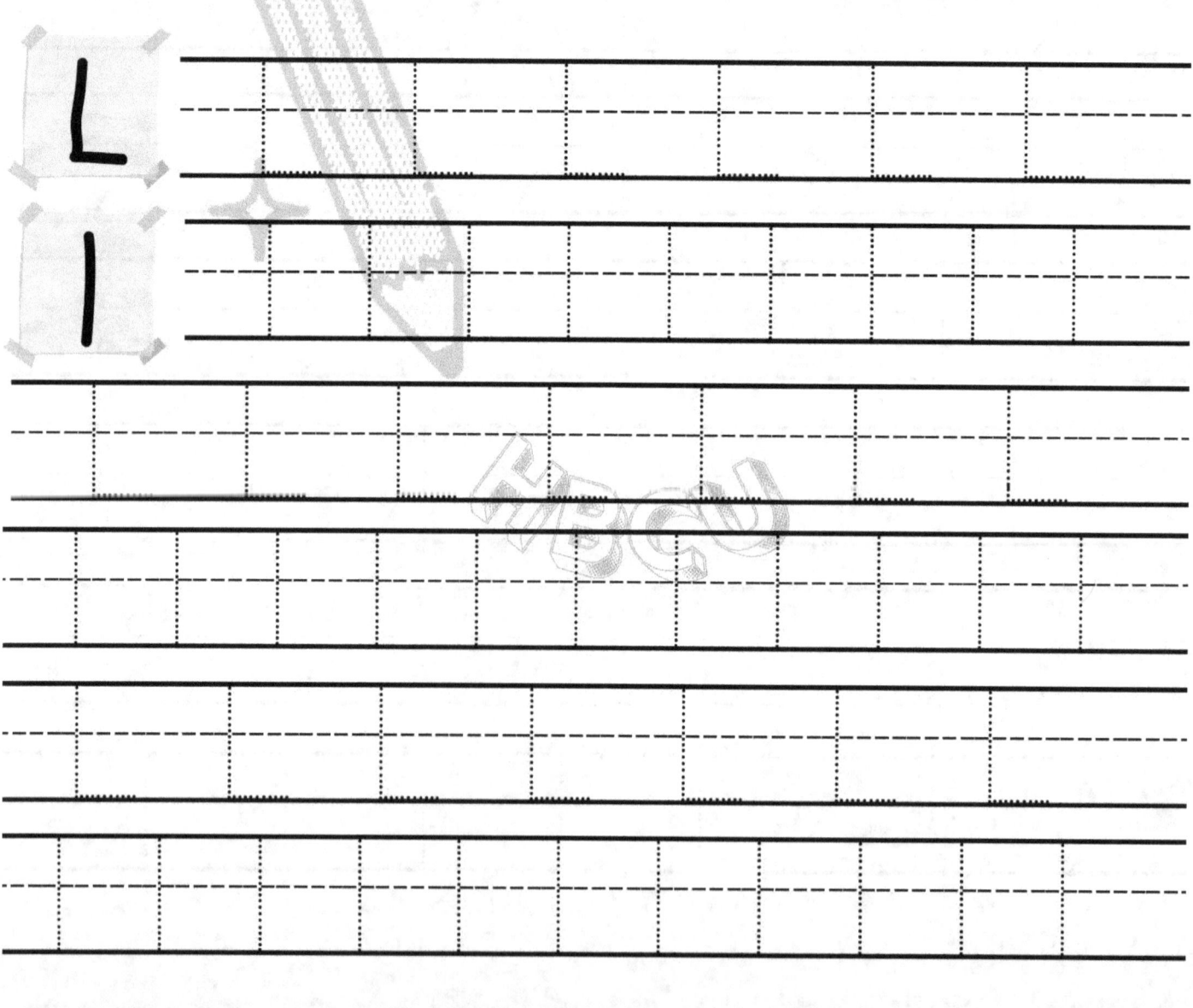

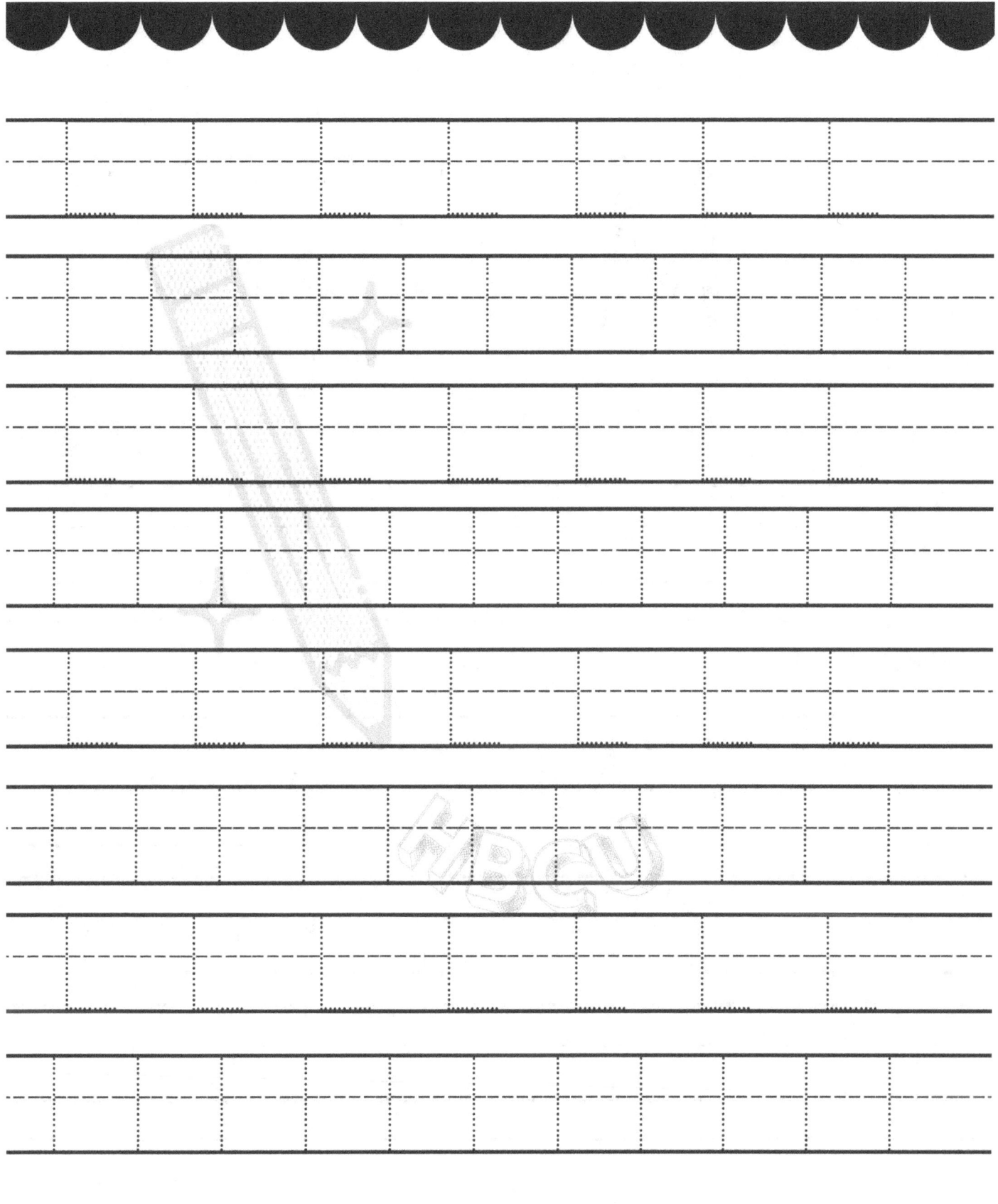

M is for

University of Maryland Eastern Shore
Meharry Medical College
Miles College
Mississippi Valley State University
Morehouse College
Morehouse School of Medicine
Morgan State University
Morris Brown College
Morris College

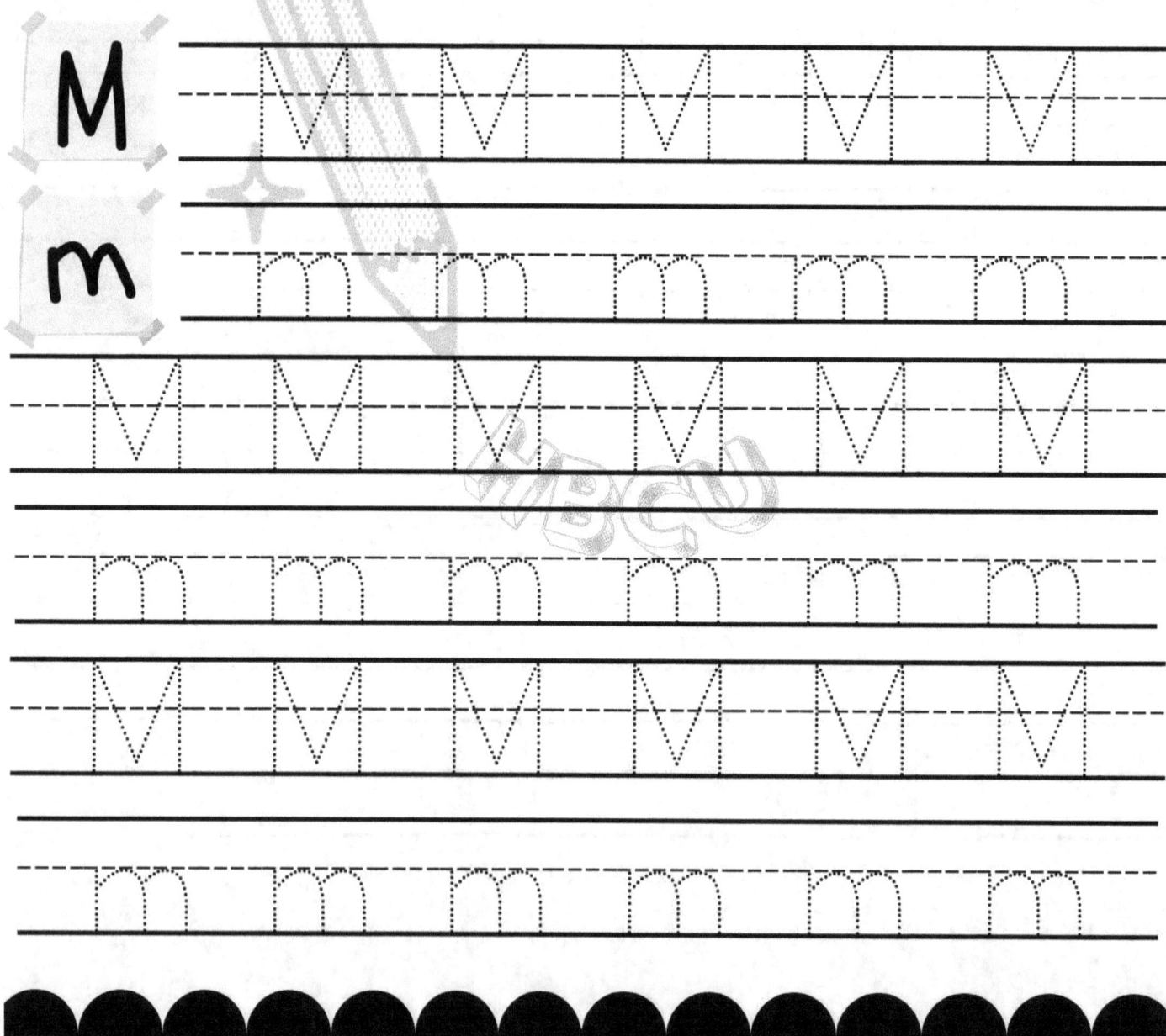

N is for
Norfolk State University
North Carolina A&T State University
North Carolina Central University

O is for Oakwood University
Omega Psi Phi Fraternity

P is for

Paine College
Paul Quinn College
Philander Smith College
Prairie View A&M University

P p

Q is for Que Dogs (Omega Psi Phi)
Queens

R is for Rust College Rivalries

S is for

- Savannah State University
- Selma University
- Shaw University
- Shelton State Community College
- Shorter College
- Simmons College of Kentucky
- South Carolina State University
- Southern University at New Orleans
- Southern University at Shreveport
- Southern University and A&M College
- Southwestern Christian College
- Spelman College
- St. Augustine's University
- St. Philip's College
- Stillman College
- Sigma Gamma Rho Sorority
- Phi Beta Sigma Fraternity
- Step shows

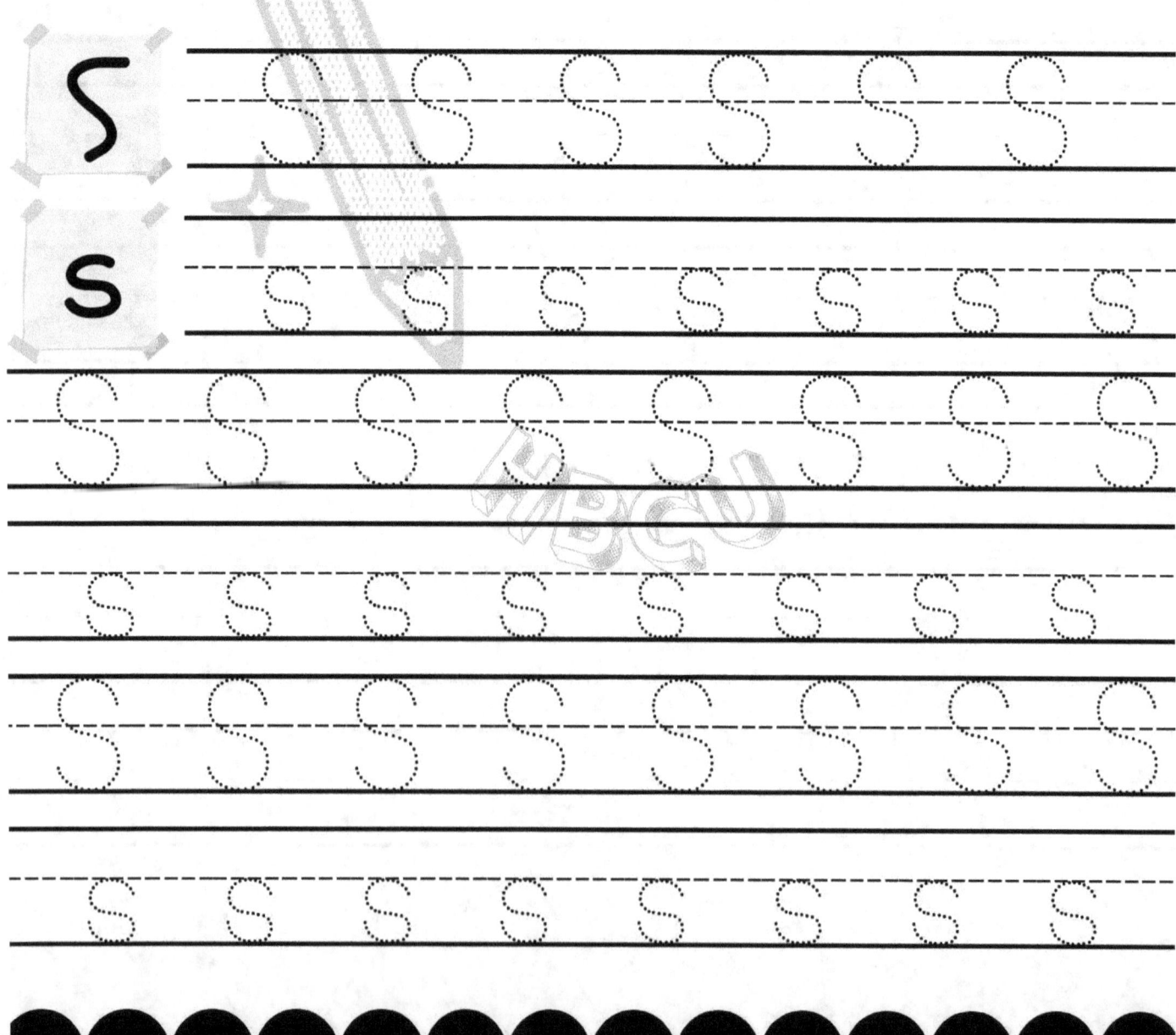

S S S S S S S S

S S S S S S S S

S S S S S S S S

S S S S S S S S

S S S S S S S S

S S S S S S S S

S S S S S S S S

S S S S S S S S

T is for

- Talladega College
- Tennessee State University
- Texas College
- Texas Southern University
- Tougaloo College
- Trenholm State Community College
- Tuskegee University

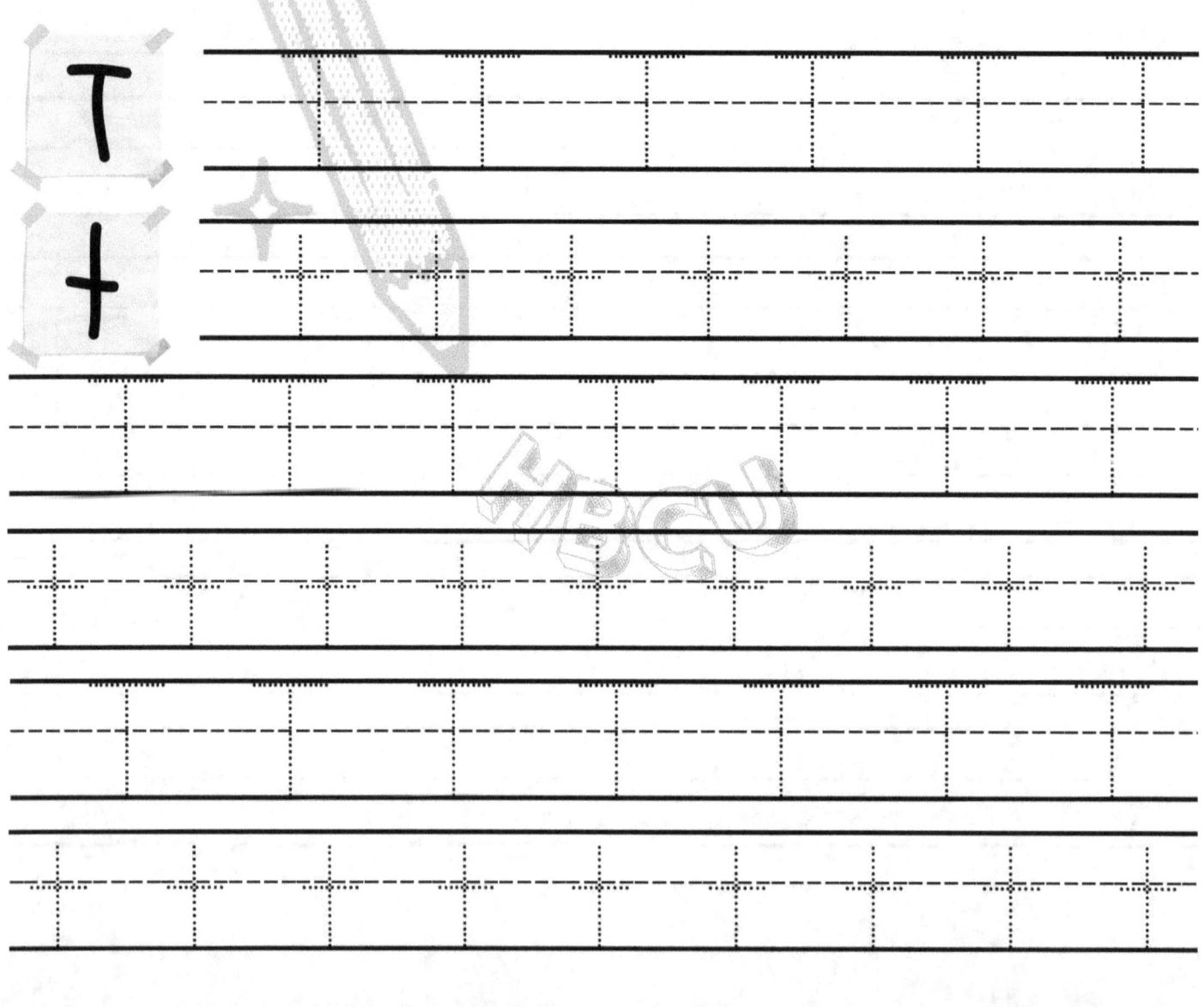

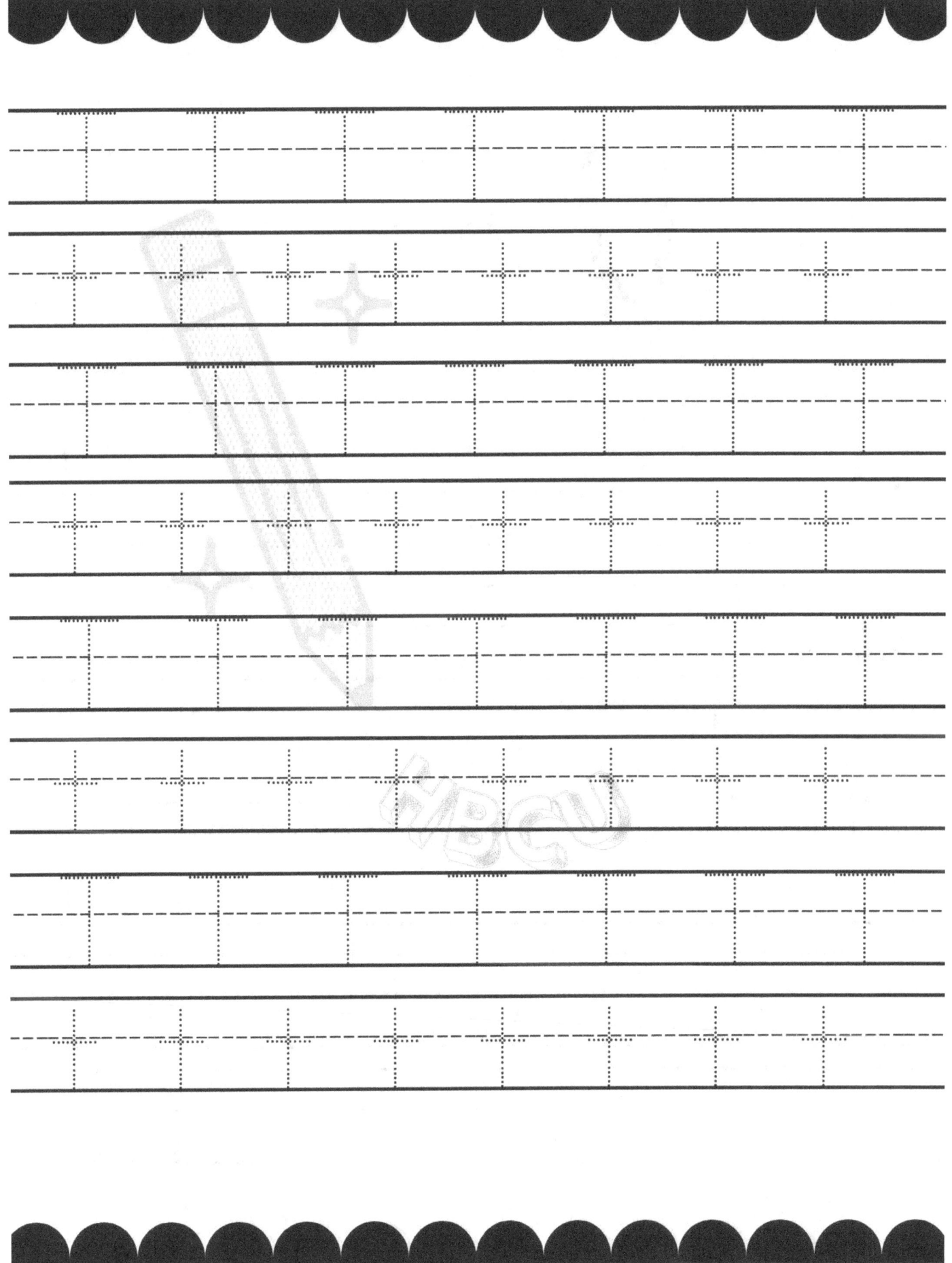

U is for University

V is for

University of the Virgin Islands
Virginia State University
Virginia Union University
Virginia University of Lynchburg
Voorhees University

W is for

West Virginia State University
Wilberforce University
Wiley College
Winston-Salem State University

X is for   Xavier University of Louisiana

Y is for Young Gifted and Black

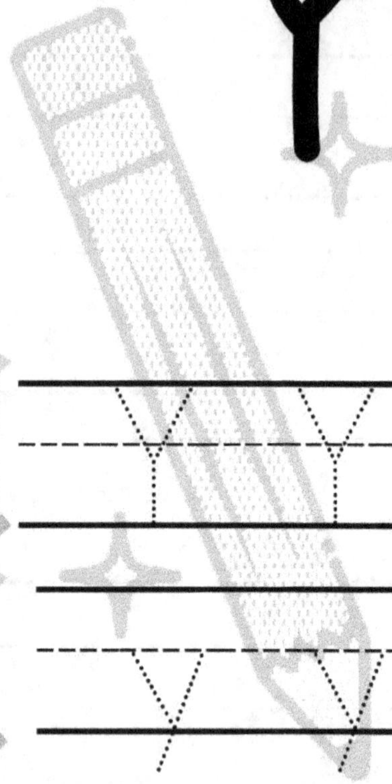

Y

y

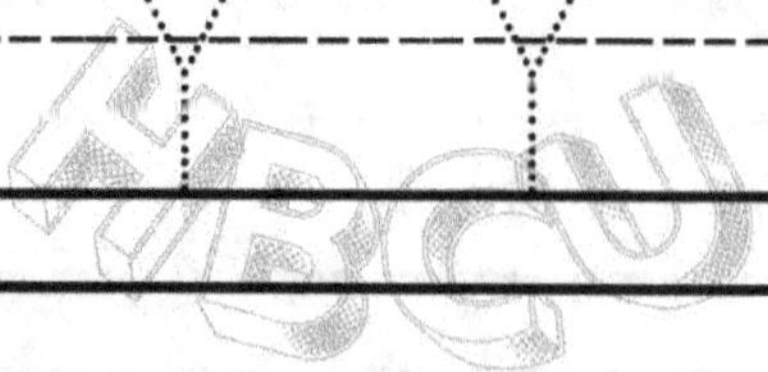

Z is for Zeta Phi Beta Sorority

www.ingramcontent.com/pod-product-compliance
Lightning Source LLC
Chambersburg PA
CBHW051215290426
44109CB00021B/2464